INCREDIBLY DISGUSTING ENVIRONMENTS™

# PESTICIDES AND YOUR BODY

Jennifer Landau

rosen publishing's
rosen
central®

New York

*For the next seven generations*

Published in 2013 by The Rosen Publishing Group, Inc.
29 East 21st Street, New York, NY 10010

First Edition

**Library of Congress Cataloging-in-Publication Data**

Landau, Jennifer, 1961-
Pesticides and your body/Jennifer Landau.
    p. cm.—(Incredibly disgusting environments)
Includes bibliographical references and index.
ISBN 978-1-4488-8413-1 (library binding)—
ISBN 978-1-4488-8422-3 (pbk.)—
ISBN 978-1-4488-8423-0 (6-pack)
1. Pesticides—Health aspects—Juvenile literature. 2. Pesticides—Environmental aspects—Juvenile literature. 3. Pesticides—Toxicology—Juvenile literature. I. Title.
RA1270.P4L36 2013
363.738'498—dc23

2012018544

*Manufactured in the United States of America*

CPSIA Compliance Information: Batch #W13YA: For further information, contact Rosen Publishing, New York, New York, at 1-800-237-9932.

# CONTENTS

# INTRODUCTION

**Have you ever seen** one of those yellow signs telling you to stay off a neighbor's lawn for twenty-four hours because the grass or trees have recently been sprayed with pesticides? Those warnings are there because pesticides, most of which are man-made chemicals, might be harmful to you. They are poisons designed to kill. In fact, the suffix "–cide" means "to kill," like in the words "suicide" (to kill yourself) or "homicide" (to kill another person). Pesticides kill bugs, weeds, mice, and other pests that destroy crops or threaten public health or simply interfere with people's desire for a weed-free front yard. Types of pesticides include the following:

Insecticides—used to destroy insects

Herbicides—used to destroy unwanted plants

Fungicides—used to destroy fungus

Rodenticides—used to destroy rodents such as rats and mice

It's true that pesticides have allowed farmers to produce a greater variety of crops at a much lower price. They have been effective in killing insects and vermin that can make people sick or damage the food supply.

The effectiveness of pesticides also makes them a potential danger to people of all ages. They work *because* they are toxic, so there are no safe pesticides when it comes to human health. That is why pesticides have to be regulated under federal and state laws to contain the risk to people and the environment.

Pesticides are used everywhere: in schools and homes and parks and playgrounds, and especially in agriculture, which means they get

PESTICIDE APPLICATION
DO NOT ENTER

DO NOT REMOVE
SIGN FOR 24 HOURS

into our food supply. The fruits and vegetables we eat carry the residue, or remains, of one or more pesticides.

These poisons are used in huge numbers, too. According to Marvin J. Levine, author of *Pesticides: A Toxic Time Bomb in Our Midst,* every year in the United States approximately 834 billion pounds (378.3 billion kilograms) of active pesticide ingredients are released into the environment. That's more than 4 pounds (1.8 kg) per person annually. Pesticides are used in sixty-nine million homes and on nine hundred thousand farms.

Companies that spray toxic pesticides have to post signs warning people to stay away from the area for twenty-four hours. They should also keep children and pets from the area.

All those toxins get into the air and water and soil. Many remain there long after those yellow warning signs are removed from someone's lawn. They get into bodies beginning in the womb, and the poisons are passed down from mother to child. They remain a lifelong threat for children, teens, adults, the elderly, and even people's pets.

As you read on, you'll see how pesticides became so popular in this country and learn the many ways they can damage human health, both in the short term and the long term. Illnesses such as asthma and cancer are linked to pesticides. So are developmental problems like attention-deficit/hyperactivity disorder (ADHD), autism, and lowered IQ. Some pesticides can even affect your ability to produce children and, for women, to carry children to term.

There is good reason to be concerned about what pesticides are doing to people's bodies. However, you'll also learn that there are steps you can take to protect yourself, your family, and your community from these dangerous chemicals.

# 1 EVERYONE AT RISK

**Pesticides are designed to be toxic**. If they don't kill, they are not doing their job. The problem is that while these pesticides are targeting weeds or insects or rats, they are also poisoning the environment. This can affect your health.

You can be exposed to pesticides by breathing them in, getting them in your mouth or digestive tract, or by contact with your eyes or skin. People eat food sprayed with pesticides, go to schools where the buildings and grounds are treated with pesticides, and shop at malls where the trees in the parking lot have been sprayed.

If you don't see how this might affect you, consider the following: In 2011, *Consumer Reports*, a magazine that checks the safety and effectiveness of products, tested eighty-eight samples of apple and grape juice for arsenic, a chemical that is found organically in the soil, but also used in pesticides, as well as paint and wood preservatives. Arsenic is a known carcinogen, or cancer-causing agent. *Consumer Reports* found that 10 percent of

the juices contained arsenic levels that exceeded the federal drinking water standards, as well as lead levels that were too high.

In February 2012, researchers at Dartmouth College found dangerous levels of arsenic in brown rice syrup, which is used to sweeten everything from baby formula to cereal bars to energy drinks. Brown rice is typically higher in inorganic arsenic, the more toxic form, because it is found on the outer layer of the grain, which is removed in its processing into white rice.

In some parts of the country, local governments send out trucks equipped with foggers that spray pesticides throughout a residential area.

The Environmental Protection Agency (EPA), which is tasked with protecting human health and the environment, set an acceptable limit of 10 parts per billion (ppb) of total arsenic—both organic and inorganic—for drinking water. According to the Dartmouth report, a soy-based formula made with brown rice syrup had a total arsenic level of 60 ppb, and an inorganic arsenic level of 22 ppb, far above the EPA limit. In an interview with ABCNews.com environmental chemist Brian P. Jackson saw this as "potentially a big public health issue that has not been taken on board."

# Poisoned from the Start

Everyone is at risk from exposure to these toxins, beginning in the womb. According to the *New York Times*, a 2010 report by the President's Cancer Panel noted that three hundred contaminants—including chemicals used in pesticides—had been found in the umbilical cord blood of newborns. The report states that these babies are being born "pre-polluted."

Young children are particularly at risk to exposure. They play on the ground more than older kids and adults and have their hands in their mouths all the time, so there's a better chance they'll take in whatever pesticides are in the environment. They are also less able to detoxify, or get rid of, the toxins that do enter their bodies. *Pesticides in the Diets of Infants and Children*, a report by the National Academy of Sciences, concluded that

50 percent of lifetime pesticide exposure occurs during the first five years of life.

Older adults have cause for concern, too. The outer layer of a person's skin thins as he or she ages, so pesticides could be absorbed more quickly. Blood flow slows as a person gets older, and the liver and kidney get smaller. This makes it harder to break down pesticides and remove them from the body.

This girl is among those protesting the aerial spraying of pesticides in parts of Northern California. Young people are especially at risk to the dangers of pesticides.

# Killer of All Killers

According to Marvin J. Levine, author of *Pesticides: A Toxic Time Bomb in Our Midst*, there are currently seventeen thousand pesticide products and more than eight hundred active ingredients registered in the United States. These are not the only dangerous ingredients in pesticides, though. Inert ingredients, which don't target the pests directly, are also a threat. Inert ingredients are added to make the pesticide more effective. They help the pesticide last longer or stick to the surface of plants and soil better, for example. Inert ingredients are chemicals, and those that have been approved include lead compounds and chemicals known to cause cancer. The scariest thing is that manufacturers aren't required to list inert ingredients on the pesticide label, so you don't necessarily know everything that is in the product.

It wasn't always this way. For thousands of years, farmers used natural means like crop rotation to get rid of pests. In crop rotation, farmers plant either more than one crop in a single field or they change the crop, making it harder for pests to find food. As the country's population grew, farmers decided to focus on just one crop because they could grow more while putting in less work. This increase meant more pests, too, so farmers turned to chemical pesticides.

The first widely used pesticide was DDT, a chlorine-based pesticide. DDT was first used in World War II (1939–1945) to kill insects that caused diseases such as typhus and malaria. In 1944, a typhus epidemic broke out in Naples, Italy, and the United States military

# THE BHOPAL DISASTER

In 1984, there was a gas leak of methyl isocyanate, a chemical used to produce pesticides, at the Union Carbide pesticide plant in Bhopal, India. The leak killed two thousand people almost immediately, and thousands more died from the aftereffects. Hundreds of thousands suffered damage from the toxic gas. The gas leak at Bhopal is considered one of the worst industrial disasters in history.

It was not until 2010 that eight former executives of the company were convicted of negligence in the case. "Negligence" means they did not take proper care to protect their employees and the citizens of Bhopal. The men received sentences of two years, which critics thought far too short. Union Carbide paid the Indian government $470 million to settle victims' claims. The accident site still has hundreds of tons of hazardous waste that has yet to be cleared, posing further health risks for the men, women, and children living in the area.

dusted more than one million people with DDT to kill the lice that carried the disease. The pesticide was so cheap and effective that people began calling it the "killer of all killers." Unfortunately, few were paying attention to what, in addition to insects, DDT was killing. There was no testing done to see the potential health effect on humans or animals.

In 1945, the U.S. government permitted the sale of DDT to the public. The use of DDT and other, even stronger, pesticides grew. Farmers found it easier to spray a field than to plow it. Families would set off DDT "bombs" in their house, and kids would run after the DDT truck as it rolled through the neighborhood. They unknowingly were inhaling the insecticide spray and poisoning their nervous systems.

# Silent Spring

Rachel Carson, a writer and biologist who worked for the U.S. Fish and Wildlife Service, had a friend who owned a bird sanctuary where planes had sprayed DDT. The insecticide was meant to kill gypsy months, which it did. It also killed thousands of songbirds

A photograph from 1945 shows people enjoying their day at a Long Island beach as a truck spraying DDT rolls by. At the time, people were unaware of the pesticide's dangerous health effects.

in the sanctuary, along with rabbits, squirrels, and even cats and dogs. Streams in forests sprayed with the insecticide left many fish dead.

DDT damaged the food supply as well. It poisoned the earthworms that robins ate, and so the birds would die after eating them. The robins that did survive had been so affected by DDT that they laid eggs with very thin shells. In fact, the shells were so thin that they cracked when the mother or father bird tried to sit on them. In this way, DDT, considered a miracle by some, destroyed multiple generations of creatures.

In 1962, Rachel Carson published *Silent Spring*, a book that many believe started the modern environmental movement. Along with the damage to wildlife, Carson noted that people who worked with the insecticide were at risk for central nervous system damage, as this was the target of the poisons. Anxiety, joint pain, or even convulsions were possible. Long-term effects included cancer and liver damage. Carson believed that not only was DDT deadly, but it also was ineffective. After

In her 1962 book *Silent Spring*, Rachel Carson warned about the damage DDT could cause to people, animals, and the environment.

a while only those pests that could resist the poisons would survive and breed future generations.

While some critics dismissed Carson, who died of breast cancer in 1964, as a crank, her work led directly to the banning of chlorine-based pesticides and to the creation of the EPA, which regulates pesticide use in the United States. In the 1994 reissue of *Silent Spring*, then-vice president Al Gore wrote that without Rachel Carson's work "the environmental movement might have been delayed or never have developed at all."

Although Carson urged caution when using pesticides like DDT, she did not ask for them to be eliminated completely. In *Silent Spring* she wrote, "Practical advice should be 'Spray as little as you possibly can' rather than 'Spray to the limit of your capacity.'" Given that tens of thousands of pesticides are still on the market, it seems as if Carson's advice has not been fully heeded.

# 2 HOW PESTICIDES CAN HARM YOUR BODY

**In 2011, a woman who worked** in a plant nursery walked into the offices of the Farmworker Association of Florida. Jeannie Economos of the Farmworker Association told the *Palm Beach Post* that the woman's face "was swollen and her eyes were almost shut…she'd been affected by pesticides."

The nursery worker was the victim of acute pesticide poisoning. Acute poisoning (also called acute toxicity) means exposure to a higher dose of a poison in a short period of time. People who work with pesticides or those who pick crops in fields that are heavily sprayed are particularly at risk. Younger people are also at risk because they are less likely to be cautious around pesticides and more likely to put their hands in their mouths or touch their eyes after exposure.

Symptoms of acute toxicity depend on the pesticide, the route of exposure—whether the pesticide was inhaled, eaten, or absorbed through the skin—and the amount taken in. These symptoms can include everything from skin and eye irritation to difficulty breathing, nausea, numbness, convulsions, and even

death. According to Marvin J. Levine's *Pesticides: A Toxic Time Bomb in Our Midst*, about fifteen to twenty death certificates per year contain codes for accidental pesticide poisoning, an estimate that is thought to be lower than the actual number of deaths tied to acute poisoning.

# Our Burdened Bodies

Chronic toxicity involves the damage that comes from being exposed to a smaller amount of pesticides over a longer

This Texas man claims that toxins released by a nearby pesticide plant caused the massive sores on his arms.

amount of time. Weeks, months, or even years can go by before the effects of this damage are seen. Chronic toxicity is related to body burden, which means how toxins like pesticides build up in people's bodies over time. Some of the many diseases associated with chronic toxicity are discussed later.

In 2007, journalist Anderson Cooper had his blood and urine tested for 246 synthetic, or man-made, chemicals. When the results came back, Cooper found that he had more than one hundred chemicals in his system! These chemicals included DDT, the insecticide Rachel Carson warned about in *Silent Spring* and one that had been banned in the United States since 1972.

The Centers for Disease Control and Prevention (CDC) released its *Fourth National Report on Human Exposure to Environmental Chemicals* in 2009. The Environmental Working Group (EWG), an advocacy organization whose goal is to protect public health and the environment, analyzed the results and found that 96 percent of the people in the study had pesticides in their blood and urine. As with Cooper, pesticides that had not been used for decades were among those detected.

# A Persistent Danger

Some pesticides are considered persistent, which means that rather than breaking down easily they stay in the environment for a long time. While most of these organochlorine pesticides (like DDT) have now been banned in the United States, the fact that

# MYTHS & FACTS

**Myth:** Only people who work with pesticides are at risk of getting sick.

**Fact:** Although those who work with pesticides on a continuous basis may be at a greater risk, these poisons are potentially dangerous to everyone. Low-dose, long-term exposure can lead to many illnesses in young children, teenagers, and adults.

**Myth:** Without pesticides, farms and homes would be overrun with insects and other pests.

**Fact:** Pesticides become less effective over time. Pests can develop resistance to the toxin, requiring more pesticides—as well as different combinations—to be applied.

**Myth:** There's no need to worry about pesticides because the government tests them all for safety.

**Fact:** Although manufacturers have to register each new pesticide with the EPA, this is not a product safety program. The EPA uses the information about a pesticide to determine how it should be labeled and applied. Also, many older pesticides still on the market are only now going through the testing that Congress began requiring in the late 1970s.

they stick around in our soil and waterways for decades makes them dangerous. That's how these chemicals still show up in the blood and urine of people who weren't even born when they were being used regularly.

The persistence of these toxins is related to the concept of bioconcentration, which is the tendency for pesticides in the environment to build up in the tissue of a body's organs. Pesticides are especially likely to accumulate in fatty tissue. In this way, pesticides in a lake, for example, build up in the fatty tissue of a fish. What's

Even after the EPA spent millions of dollars trying to remove DDT from a California harbor, the fish found there were still too contaminated with the pesticide to be safely eaten.

frightening is that the chemicals in the pesticide become more concentrated as you move up the food chain. Humans are at the top of the food chain, so we end up taking in more toxins than any other link in that chain, putting ourselves at great risk.

Another risk is pesticide synergy. This means that two pesticides mixed together might react in a way that makes the combination much stronger than simply adding one pesticide to another. Whatever testing the EPA does is on single pesticides, so there is no way of knowing how dangerous some of these mixtures could be. The EPA simply can't test every combination of the more than eight hundred active ingredients it allows manufacturers to use. According to Marvin Levine, author of *Pesticides: A Toxic Time Bomb in Our Midst*, this fact "sent a chill through the EPA, which suddenly faced the possibility that all of their safety tests were suspect."

# Jamming the Signals

To give you an idea of precisely how pesticides prevent your body from functioning properly, consider how insecticides work. These toxins are designed to target the nervous system of insects. The structure of the nervous system is similar in insects and mammals, which is why insecticides can cause great harm to humans, too.

In both humans and insects, electrical impulses help move messages along nerve cells. At the end of each nerve cell a neurotransmitter—a messenger of sorts—activates the next

# THE CHEERS STUDY

The Children's Health Environmental Exposure Research Study (CHEERS) was proposed by the EPA in 2004 as a way to measure the effects of pesticides on children. The plan was to give $970, children's clothes, and a camcorder to the families of sixty kids in a low-income, minority neighborhood in Florida that was known as a high-exposure area. While those conducting the study did not plan to increase the amount of pesticides these children would be exposed to, critics found fault with the idea of simply standing by and documenting the toxins these kids would ingest.

In addition, the EPA had agreed to accept $2 million toward the study from the American Chemistry Council, a group that represents companies that manufacture chemicals used in pesticides. Many saw this as a clear conflict of interest. Because of overwhelming criticism, the study was cancelled in 2005.

nerve cell in the chain of cells. This nerve cell then removes any neurotransmitters left from previous signals, clearing the pathway.

One important neurotransmitter is called acetylcholine, which is broken down by the enzyme acetylcholinesterase. Two major types of insecticides prevent this enzyme from working, which results in the neurotransmitter not getting broken down properly at the end of a nerve cell. What follows is a jamming of the signals from one nerve cell to the next. Depending on the amount of

pesticide ingested, this can cause symptoms that range from head-aches and nausea to seizures and, in extreme cases, even death.

This jamming of signals affects the endocrine system, which controls the release of hormones. These are chemicals produced by our bodies to control and regulate our physical, sexual, and mental growth. Hormones are vital in early development and in reproduction, so by interfering with this process pesticides can cause harm to both babies in the womb and children.

Milkweed bugs exposed to pesticides have not developed normally.

# 3 HEALTH EFFECTS OF PESTICIDE USE

**In her book** *Raising Elijah: Protecting Our Children in an Age of Environmental Crisis*, ecologist Sandra Steingraber compares the environmental crisis to a tree with two branches. One branch stands for what is happening to the planet through the buildup of heat-trapping gases like carbon dioxide and methane. The other branch is what is happening to people through the buildup of toxins in their bodies.

Steingraber is herself a survivor of bladder cancer, diagnosed when she was in her twenties. She attributes her cancer to arsenic exposure when she was growing up in her hometown in Illinois. There was an apparent cancer cluster in this town, meaning more than the expected number of people developed bladder and other types of cancer.

In *Raising Elijah*, Steingraber calls one class of pesticides—the organophosphates—"brain-addling chemicals" because they cause a person's thoughts to become confused. The disorders discussed below show some of the ways pesticides can damage the body and the mind.

# Asthma

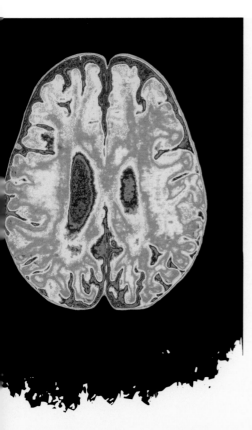

According to the American Academy of Allergy Asthma and Immunology Web site, about 300 million people around the world suffer from asthma, with 250,000 dying every year from this respiratory disease. A report from the CDC listed asthma as the third leading cause of hospitalizations in 2005 for those under the age of fifteen.

Genes play a part in whether someone develops asthma. So do environmental factors such as allergens and pollutants, including pesticides. These pollutants can be an underlying cause for asthma or can trigger an attack in someone already living with the disease.

A 2004 study published in *Environmental Health Perspectives* found that children exposed to herbicides during their first year were four and half times more likely to get an asthma diagnosis before they turned five, a diagnosis that stayed with them through the teen years and beyond. In 2002, researchers at Johns Hopkins University discovered that pesticides can trigger

A magnetic resonance imaging (MRI) scan of a man's brain shows the organophosphate damage caused by long-term exposure to pesticides. The central areas of pink and red have become very enlarged, which is a sign of poisoning.

an asthma attack by causing the airway to contract, restricting the flow of air to the lungs.

# Cancer

In 2010, the President's Cancer Panel report concluded: "[t]he entire U.S. population is exposed on a daily basis to numerous agricultural chemicals...Many of these chemicals are known or suspected of having either carcinogenic [cancer-causing] or endocrine [gland and hormone]-disrupting properties."

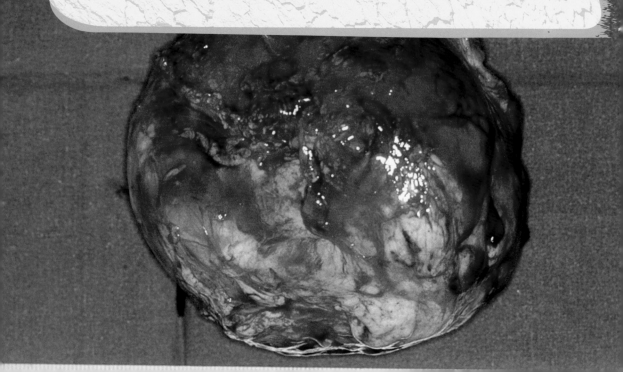

A surgeon removed this Wilms' tumor from a child's kidney. Pesticides have been linked to the development of this type of cancer.

For years, federal agencies and institutes have stated that environmental pollutants are responsible for only about 2 percent of all cancers, a number the Cancer Panel thought was very much out of date. The panel went on to criticize the chemical industry for using those low figures to "justify its claims that specific products pose little or no cancer risk."

Many cancers have been linked to pesticide use. According to the President's Cancer Panel report, chemicals in pesticides have

## PETS AT RISK

Pets can get sick from pesticides, too. A 2004 study published in the *Journal of the American Veterinary Medicine Association* found that Scottish terriers exposed to herbicide-treated lawns were four to seven times more likely to get bladder cancer. Scottish terriers are especially sensitive to their environment in relation to other breeds and require less exposure to pesticides before developing cancer. This makes them excellent sentinel animals, meaning they can serve as warnings to let scientists know the risks certain toxins pose for humans and other animals.

Another concern is products designed to kill fleas and ticks on dogs and cats. These spot-on pesticide products, applied directly to the animal's fur, have resulted in reactions ranging from skin irritation to seizures to death. In 2008, more than forty-four thousand adverse, or undesirable, side effects were reported. The EPA investigated these incidents and is working toward both tighter restrictions and better labeling on these products.

been linked to lung, kidney, stomach, and breast cancer, as well as cancers of the blood and lymph nodes. Several studies show that having a parent who works on a farm increases the risk that young people will develop brain cancer, bone cancer, and Wilms' tumor, a particular type of kidney cancer.

A 2012 Danish study strengthened the link between pesticide exposure and non-Hodgkin's lymphoma, a cancer of the lymph nodes. Researchers collected samples of fat tissue from 239 men and women in the general population. The study, published in *Environmental Health Perspectives*, showed that those who had higher levels of pesticides in their fat tissue were more likely to develop non-Hodgkin's lymphoma over time. Some of the people with high levels of pesticides in their tissue weren't diagnosed until as much as fifteen years after their samples were collected.

# Learning/Developmental Issues and Birth Defects

In 2011, the *New York Times* reported that three studies found a link between high levels of pesticide exposure when a baby was in the womb and a lower IQ once that child reached school age. In one study, every tenfold increase in exposure to a particular class of pesticide led to a five-and-a-half point drop in overall IQ scores. Dr. Philip Landrigan, director of the Children's Environmental Health Center at New York's Mount Sinai Hospital, told the *Times* that "[b]abies exposed to the highest levels had the most severe effects. It means these children are going to have problems as they go through life."

Pesticides have been targeted in many other developmental concerns, from birth defects to underdeveloped motor skills to attention deficit/hyperactivity disorder (ADHD) to autism. A 2011 study published in *Pediatrics* showed that kids between the ages of eight and fifteen who had higher levels of organophosphates in their urine were more likely to be diagnosed with ADHD.

In rare cases, the hazardous effects of pesticide can be extreme. In 2011, the *Palm Beach Post* reported on a case where parents working for a produce grower in Florida were exposed to freshly sprayed pesticides. Within six weeks of each other, three women gave birth to babies with severe birth defects, including one baby who was born without arms or legs.

# Reproductive Health

On its Web site, the Association of Reproductive Health Professionals lists several potential health effects of chronic pesticide exposure. These include reduced fertility (the ability to produce offspring), premature birth, and both early and late pregnancy loss in females. For males the risks include reduced fertility, a change in how their hormones work, and a lowered sperm count. As it can take years to determine to what extent pesticides might be damaging your health, exposure as a teen could affect you or your child when it comes time to start a family.

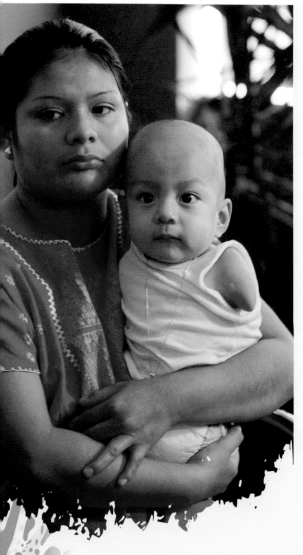

Reproductive health is related to how pesticides harm the endocrine system. Pesticides act as endocrine-disruptors, affecting both the female hormones (estrogen) and the male hormones (androgens) in negative ways. According to its Web site, the EPA believes there is "compelling evidence" that pesticides disrupt the endocrine system of fish and wildlife, "resulting in developmental and reproductive problems." The EPA is currently in the process of screening chemicals, including pesticides, for their effects on this vital system of glands and hormones.

A large produce company settled a lawsuit with this woman after she accused the company of exposing her to high levels of pesticides while she worked in the fields, causing her baby to be born without arms or legs.

# 10 GREAT QUESTIONS
## TO ASK AN ENVIRONMENTALIST

**1.** If we get rid of pesticides, won't diseases like typhus come back?

**2.** Is there a way to remove pesticide residues from fruits and vegetables before eating them?

**3.** Will eating mostly organic food protect me from pesticides?

**4.** How can I tell if pesticides are in my drinking water?

**5.** Are pesticides related to other environmental problems like climate change?

**6.** How can I know for sure that the pesticides in my blood and urine are affecting my health?

**7.** Are pesticides the only chemicals that can harm my body?

**8.** If genetically modified organisms (GMOs) are bad for your health, why does the government allow them to be sold?

**9.** Will there ever be a time when chemical pesticides are no longer needed?

**10.** Have environmental groups made any difference when it comes to protecting people from pesticides?

# 4 FINDING A SAFER WAY

**It's easy to feel discouraged** after reading about all the ways pesticides can damage your health. If every person comes into this world "pre-polluted" by pesticides and other chemicals, is it even worth trying to make things better?

Absolutely! It's not too late to make a difference for your generation and generations to come. It all begins with a change in attitude. Educate your family, friends, and school officials about the dangers of a "spray first, ask questions later" policy. It's important to stress that not every bug needs to be drowned in insecticide or every weed drenched in herbicide.

Learning about how to deal with pests in a safer, more environmentally friendly way is essential for everyone. As you read on, you'll find out about federal laws designed to protect people's health from toxins such as pesticides and discover the advantages of eating an organic diet. There is strong evidence linking pesticides with many diseases and disorders. The fight to find a better way of living has to be equally strong.

# Integrated Pest Management

Integrated pest management (IPM) is an approach to dealing with pests rather than one specific tactic. IPM can be used on farms, in homes, at schools, or anywhere that insects and other pests need to be managed. Its major principles include the following:

**Action levels:** As part of IPM, you determine beforehand when pest control action should be taken. This is often the point

A University of Minnesota researcher checks on insect traps set as part of an integrated pest management (IPM) program.

at which a pest becomes a health hazard or threatens to damage the food supply.

**Monitoring:** Monitoring and identifying pests helps determine what can be done to prevent them from becoming a threat. In combination with set action levels, this can stop people from using pesticides incorrectly or when they are not needed at all.

**Prevention:** The key to prevention is removing conditions that attract pests. This involves everything from covering cracks in a building so that rodents can't enter to planting flowers and bushes close together to give weeds less room to grow. On a farm, prevention methods include rotating different crops and plowing the soil to bury both weeds and the remains of previous crops.

**Control:** When preventative measures are not enough to keep pests in check, a way to control them must be determined.

Organic produce cannot be sprayed with conventional pesticides, but biological pesticides are permitted.

If chemical pesticides are used, it is often in combination with other methods that are less of a health risk. Biological pesticides rely on natural bacteria or insects to fight pests rather than chemicals.

# Is Organic Better?

If you want to avoid food that is treated with conventional pesticides, then going organic may be the better choice. For the U.S. Department of Agriculture (USDA) to label food organic, it has to be grown without conventional pesticides, although biological pesticides are allowed.

Organic food is more expensive, however, so if you need to limit how much you buy, watch out for produce that is heavily sprayed, such as that listed in the sidebar on page 36.

Foods derived from genetically modified organisms can't be called organic, either. GMOs are very controversial because their DNA has been altered in a lab to bring out a particular trait. For example, one of the GMO corn varieties is engineered to resist a powerful herbicide so that it can be sprayed on weeds without

# THE DIRTY DOZEN AND THE CLEAN FIFTEEN

The Environmental Working Group is an advocacy organization whose goal is to protect public health and the environment. It puts out a shopper's guide that ranks the twelve most heavily sprayed fruits and vegetables (the Dirty Dozen), with number one representing the worst of the twelve and number twelve the least contaminated of this group. In 2011, the Dirty Dozen were:

1. apples
2. celery
3. strawberries
4. peaches
5. spinach
6. nectarines (imported)
7. grapes (imported)
8. sweet bell peppers
9. potatoes
10. blueberries (domestic)
11. lettuce
12. kale/collard greens

The Clean Fifteen are those lowest in pesticides, with number one representing the best of the best:

1. onions
2. sweet corn (not GMO)
3. pineapples
4. avocado
5. asparagus
6. sweet peas
7. mangoes
8. eggplant
9. cantaloupe (domestic)
10. kiwi
11. cabbage
12. watermelon
13. sweet potatoes
14. grapefruit
15. mushrooms

harming the corn crop itself. Critics fear that this leads to over-spraying of surrounding fields, leaving only the genetically modified crops—sometimes nicknamed "Frankenfoods"—standing.

There is evidence that GMOs are a threat to human and animal health. A 2009 report from the *International Journal of Biological Sciences* found that three kinds of corn genetically modified by the Monsanto Corporation caused organ damage to rats, particularly to the liver and kidney. The authors of the report concluded: "These substances have never before been an integral part of the human or animal diet and therefore their health consequences for those who consume them, especially over long time periods are currently unknown."

Of course, simply choosing organic food is not a guarantee of good health. You have to eat wisely overall as well, choosing pears over potato chips and spinach over soda. According to the CDC, more than a third of adults in the United States are obese, as well as 17 percent of children and adolescents between the ages of two and nineteen. This obesity epidemic brings with it disorders such as type 2 diabetes, heart disease, and certain cancers. To protect our health, we have to be willing to make the necessary dietary and lifestyle changes.

# Legal Protections

Beginning in the early 1990s, there have been several laws that deal with pesticide use in the United States. The first laws were more concerned with how effectively pesticides worked rather than their safety. The Federal Insecticide, Fungicide, and Rodenticide Act (FIFRA), first passed in the 1940s and amended many times, became increasingly focused on how pesticides affected human health and the environment.

A landmark law was the Food Quality Protection Act (FQPA), passed in 1996. The FQPA, which many environmental groups worked hard to push through Congress, strengthened existing laws, especially when it came to children's health. These changes included:

- Raising the safety standard that pesticides have to meet before they are approved for use.
- Requiring that the EPA consider the combined risk from all sources (for example, food, water, and products used in the home and garden) when setting limits on pesticide levels.
- Acknowledging the increased sensitivity of infants and children to pesticides, and adding in as much as a tenfold safety factor when determining the health risks of each pesticide. For example, if the previous tolerance for pesticides on bananas was 100 ppm, the new law would require a tolerance of only 10 ppm.

Some organizations have criticized how the EPA has handled this law since it was passed. For example, the National Resources Defense Council (NRDC), an environmental group, stated on its Web site that in 2006 the tenfold safety factor had been applied to only eleven of the fifty-nine pesticides the EPA evaluated.

# Hope for a Healthier Future

Government regulation is important, but so are the everyday changes that you and your friends and family can make. Why not start a garden club at school or in your neighborhood? Focus on plants that thrive in your local area, as they are less likely to need pesticides. You can be part of a pest patrol, too, searching your

For their science fair project, two Florida teens tested pesticide levels at a nearby elementary school and found that they were elevated. As a result of this project, the Florida Department of Agriculture launched a program to instruct Florida farmers on how to reduce the risks of spraying pesticides near schools.

school for trash that's piling up or cracks that need to be sealed. Suggest that your school limit the areas where food can be eaten. The best way to keep bugs out of the classroom is to keep food out, too.

According to the *New York Times*, Rachel Carson stated in a 1963 interview with *CBS Reports* that "man's attitude toward nature is today critically important because we have now acquired a fateful power to alter and destroy nature. But man is part of nature, and his war against nature is inevitably a war against himself." Nearly fifty years later, you can see the toll this war has taken on human health. It is up to everyone to work toward a cleaner and healthier future.

# GLOSSARY

**advocacy** Actively supporting a particular issue or cause.

**contaminated** Made impure by being mixed with something harmful or dirty.

**convulsions** Severe and involuntary muscle contractions caused by high fevers or acute poisoning.

**enzyme** A protein in living cells that can produce a certain chemical reaction.

**epidemic** A disease that affects many people in an area at the same time.

**hazardous waste** Material left over when chemicals are made that can harm the environment and human health.

**malaria** A disease carried by mosquitoes that is widespread in tropical and subtropical areas of the world.

**preservatives** Chemicals and other additives meant to make substances last longer.

**sanctuary** A protected area where animals, particularly birds, can live and reproduce.

**typhus** An infectious disease carried by fleas and lice and known for its high fevers, rashes, and headaches.

**umbilical cord** The cord that connects a fetus in the womb to the mother.

**vermin** Animals or insects that cause harm to crops or carry diseases.

# FOR MORE INFORMATION

**Beyond Pesticides**

701 E Street SE, #200

Washington, DC 20003

(202) 543-5450

Web site: http://www.beyondpesticides.org

*Beyond Pesticides provides information on the health risks of pesticides and offers consumers and community-based groups nonchemical methods to get rid of pests.*

**Canadian Environmental Law Association**

130 Spadina Avenue, Suite 301

Toronto, ON M5V 2L4

Canada

(416) 960-2284

Web site: http://www.cela.ca

*The Web site of the Canadian Environmental Law Association offers many publications concerned with protecting human health and the environment.*

**Environmental Working Group (EWG)**

1436 U Street NW, Suite 100

Washington, DC 20009

(202) 667-6982

Web site: http://www.ewg.org

*The EWG provides a safety database on beauty products, a national drinking water database, and a shopper's guide to pesticides in produce.*

**Healthy Schools Network, Inc.**

773 Madison Avenue

Albany, NY 12208

(518) 462-0632

Web site: http://www.healthyschools.org

*The Healthy Schools Network offers fact sheets, posters, and reports on green cleaning, integrated pest management, and other issues related to the environmental health of school buildings and grounds.*

**Natural Resources Defense Council (NRDC)**

40 West Twentieth Street

New York, NY 10011

(212) 727-2700

Web site: http://www.nrdc.org

*The NRDC gives citizens a chance to take action to help safeguard the earth from environmental problems, including those related to pesticides.*

# Web Sites

Due to the changing nature of Internet links, Rosen Publishing has developed an online list of Web sites related to the subject of this book. This site is updated regularly. Please use this link to access the list:

http://www.rosenlinks.com/IDE/Pest

# FOR FURTHER READING

Bouchard, Maryse F., David C. Bellinger, Robin O. Wright, and Marc G. Weisskop. "Attention-Deficit/Hyperactivity Disorder and Urinary Metabolites of Organophosphate Pesticides." *Pediatrics* 125 (6), 2010.

Bråuner, Elvira Vaclavik, Mette Sørensen, Eric Gaudreau, Alain LeBlanc, Kirsten Thorup Eriksen, Anne Tjønneland, Kim Overad, and Ole Raaschou-Nielsen. "A Prospective Study of Organochlorines in Adipose Tissue and Risk on Non-Hodgkin Lymphoma." *Environmental Health Perspectives* 120 (1), 2012.

Carson, Rachel. *Silent Spring. Boston,* MA: Houghton Mifflin Company, 2002.

Centers for Disease Control and Prevention. *The Fourth National Report on Human Exposure to Environmental Chemicals.* Atlanta, GA: Centers for Disease Control and Prevention.

Environmental Working Group. *Shopper's Guide to Pesticides in Produce.* Retrieved March 1, 2012 (http://www.ewg.org/foodnews/guide).

Field, M. "Asthma, the Breathtaking Disease." *Magazine of Johns Hopkins Bloomberg School of Public Heath.* Retrieved March 6, 2012 (http://www.jhsph.edu/publichealthnews/magazine/archive/mag_fall02/asthma.html).

Glickman, Lawrence T., Malathi Raghavan, Deborah W. Knapp, Patty L. Bonney, and Marcia H. Dawson. "Herbicide Exposure and the Risk of Transitional Cell Carcinoma of the Urinary Bladder in Scottish Terriers." *Journal of the American Veterinary Medical Association.* 224 (8), April 2004.

Lantigua, John. "Florida Farmworkers Urge EPA to Tighten Control of Pesticides." *Palm Beach Post*, December 6, 2011. Retrieved March 22, 2012 (http://www.palmbeachpost.com/news/florida-farmworkers-urge-epa-to-tighten-control-of-2014429.html).

Leffall, Lasalle D., and Margaret L. Kripke. *The President's Cancer Panel 2008-2009 Annual Report.* Washington, D.C.: National Cancer Institute, 2010. Retrieved March 11, 2012 (http://deainfo.nci.nih.gov/advisory/pcp/annualreports/pcp08-09rpt/PCP_Report_08-09_508.pdf).

Leonard, Jonathan Norton. "Rachel Carson Dies of Cancer, 'Silent Spring' Author Was 56." *New York Times*, April 15, 1964. Retrieved March 12, 2012 (http://www.nytimes.com/books/97/10/05/reviews/carson-obit.html?_r=2).

Levine, Marvin J. *Pesticides: A Toxic Time Bomb in Our Midst.* Westport, CT: Praeger Publishers, 2007.

Parker-Pope, Tara. "Pesticide Exposure in Womb Affects I.Q." *New York Times*, April 21, 2011.

Spiroux de Vendômois, Joël, François Roullier, Dominque Cellier, and Gilles-Eric Séralini. "A Comparison of the Effects of Three GMO Corn Varieties on Mammalian Health." *International Journal of Biological Sciences* 5(7), 2009.

Steingraber, Sandra. Raising *Elijah: Protecting Our Children in an Age of Environmental Crisis.* Boston, MA: Da Capo Press, 2011.

# BIBLIOGRAPHY

Amsel, Sheri. *365 Ways to Live Green for Kids: Saving the Environment at Home, School, or at Play—Every Day.* Avon, MA: Adams Media, 2009.

Belli, Brita. *The Autism Puzzle: Connecting the Dots Between Environmental Toxins and Rising Autism Rates.* New York, NY: Seven Stories Press, 2012.

Gavigan, Christopher. *Healthy Child, Healthy World: Creating a Cleaner, Greener, Safer Home.* New York, NY: Dutton/Penguin, 2008.

Greer, Beth. *Super Natural Home: Improve Your Health, Home, and Planet—One Room at a Time.* Emmaus, PA: Rodale Books, 2009.

Jakab, Cheryl. *Pollution.* Tarrytown, NY: Marshall Cavendish, 2010.

Javna, Sophie. *The New 50 Simple Things Kids Can Do to Save the Earth.* Kansas City, MO: Andrews McMeel Publishing, 2009.

Jenkins, McKay. *What's Gotten into Us?: Staying Healthy in a Toxic World.* New York, NY: Random House, 2011.

Lear, Linda. *Rachel Carson: Witness for Nature.* Boston, MA: Mariner Books, 2009.

Natterson, Cara. *Dangerous or Safe?: Which Foods, Medicines, and Chemicals Really Put Your Kids at Risk.* New York, NY: Hudson Street Press/Penguin, 2009.

Pollan, Michael. *The Omnivore's Dilemma for Kids: The Secrets Behind What You Eat.* New York, NY: Dial Books, 2009.

Weir, Theresa. *The Orchard.* New York, NY: Grand Central Publishing, 2011.

# INDEX

# About the Author

Jennifer Landau received her M.A. in creative writing from New York University and her M.S.T. in general and special education from Fordham University. Besides her work as a special education teacher, Landau has taught writing to high school students. As a mother, she has a vested interest in the ways in which genes and the environment interact to play a part in health and developmental issues. She is particularly concerned with keeping schools free from pesticides and other toxins.

# Photo Credits